TOP 10
NASCAR
DRIVERS

Gail Blasser Riley

SPORTS
TOP 10

ENSLOW PUBLISHERS, INC.

44 Fadem Rd.	P.O. Box 38
Box 699	Aldershot
Springfield, N.J. 07081	Hants GU12 6BP
U.S.A.	U.K.

Dedication
To my sister, Linda, with love

Acknowledgments
The author would like to offer special thanks to:
Mike Meadows, Jerry Markland, and Bob Costanzo—Photographic Services
Department, Daytona International Speedway.
Dave Rodman, Director of Public Relations—Daytona International Speedway.
Martha Jane Bonkemeyer—Petty Enterprises.
Wanette Musser—NASCAR Public Relations.
National Association of Stock Car Automobile Racing.
Donnie Johnson, for courtesy and assistance.
My family, for love and patience.
Linda Blasser Martin, for encouragement and enthusiastic clarification.
Babs Bell Hajdusiewicz, for expert assistance in matters of editing, revising,
and friendship.

Library of Congress Cataloging-in-Publication Data

Riley, Gail Blasser.
   Top 10 NASCAR drivers / Gail Blasser Riley
       p. cm.—(Sports top 10)
   Includes index.
   ISBN 0-89490-611-9
     1. Automobile racing drivers—Biography—Juvenile literature.
2. NASCAR (Association)—Juvenile literature. [1. Automobile
racing drivers. 2. NASCAR (Association)] I. Title. II. Title:
Top ten NASCAR drivers. III. Series.
GV1032.A1R55 1995
796.7'2'0922—dc20
   [B]   94–32061
                                              CIP
                                              AC

Printed in the United States of America

10 9 8 7 6 5 4 3

Photo Credits: Courtesy of Daytona International Speedway, pp. 6, 9, 10, 13, 14, 17,
18, 21, 22, 25, 26, 29, 30, 33, 34, 37, 38 41, 42, 45.

Cover Photo: Courtesy of Daytona International Speedway.

Interior Design: Richard Stalzer

CONTENTS

Introduction

CHOOSING THE BEST OF THE BEST—what a difficult task! Narrowing the field to only ten NASCAR drivers for this book was challenging, to say the least. In selecting my top ten drivers, I took many factors into account.

Not only did I consider race action, but I also looked at the drivers away from the track. Work to improve the image of the sport, community involvement, contribution to charities, work for children, and attitude toward the fans—these were all important as I worked toward a decision.

In considering race action, I thought about some very impressive qualities each of these ten racers had to offer. These include strategy, nerve, speed, guts, spunk, driving ability, determination, caution, fighting spirit, ability to win record purses, and ability to come out on top without intentionally bumping other cars off the track.

Though I have chosen ten racers, these are only my personal selections. With so many NASCAR greats, it was very difficult to limit the number. Many drivers could easily have been included, and if others had written this book, they might have come up with a different mix. Perhaps you have a list of your own favorites. I hope you'll see some of them here.

CAREER STATISTICS

Driver	Wins	Top 5	Top 10	Career Winnings	Pole Positions
BOBBY ALLISON	84	319	441	$7,102,233	57
NEIL BONNETT	18	83	154	$3,861,661	20
SARA CHRISTIAN	N/A	1	2	$600	0
BILL ELLIOTT	40	151	272	$19,236,132	49
STERLING MARLIN	6	56	146	$11,403,067	9
BENNY PARSONS	21	199	283	$3,926,539	20
RICHARD PETTY*	200	550	693	$7,757,409	127
FIREBALL ROBERTS**	32	93	131	$325,349	33
DARRELL WALTRIP	84	276	390	$17,123,060	59
CALE YARBOROUGH	83	255	318	$5,003,716	70

Win statistics courtesy of NASCAR

*Petty Win Statistics:
Courtesy of Petty
Enterprises.
**Roberts win statistics:
Gregory Lawrence Fielden,
Forty Years of Stock Car Racing,
Volumes I & IV

BOBBY ALLISON

Bobby Allison won the title "Most Popular Driver" seven times in his racing career.

A MAZE OF COLORS ZOOMED past the grandstand at Talladega. Thousands cheered as the forty-one cars zipped around the track. Bobby Allison's Buick raced behind his son Davey's Ford. Bobby concentrated. He whipped through the middle of the dogleg on the front stretch. He gripped the steering wheel.

Suddenly, he was airborne! In the air, his car flipped end over end toward the protective fence at 210 miles per hour. The Buick sliced through the fence like a knife through butter, and dragged a section of the metal onto the track. Pieces of fence and car flew wildly through the air as the Buick finally came to rest.

Davey watched anxiously in his rearview mirror. After he saw his dad crawl safely out of the car and the track was cleared of wreckage, Davey went on to win the 1987 Winston 500. As a result of Bobby Allison's crash, NASCAR officials began to see that cars hurtling through the air so fast are very much like airplanes. Officials now require a carburetor restrictor plate at Talladega and Daytona to reduce speed.

When Bobby Allison spun off the track that day in 1987, perhaps his thoughts were spinning back to 1966 when he surprised everyone by taking first place in a lightweight Chevrolet with a small engine. Few believed the small car had a chance, but as Allison put it: "It handled well right off the trailer. And . . . it blew right by all the hot dogs."[1]

During the 1972 season, Richard Petty and Bobby Allison butted heads and fenders again and again. The season focused on these two drivers. Their race at Martinsville Speedway was even called "an automotive boxing match."[2] Some say it was one of the greatest races of all time. Allison started on the pole. His Chevy ran in front for 432 of the 500 laps. At one point, Petty came off the wall and slammed into Allison. Allison's fuel cap was knocked loose. In the end, Allison came in second, only six seconds behind Petty.

Allison, however, bested Petty and took first in ten of the races the two fought in 1972.

In the 1972 Winston Cup Grand National Division, Bobby Allison won almost $350,000. He finished just under the top, second in points only to Richard Petty. In later seasons, Allison went on to finish first or second time and time again. By 1988, he had won more money than Petty. But that same year, a crash at Pocono Raceway almost killed him. Bobby Allison decided to stop racing, but he stayed in the sport as a car owner.

Bobby Allison has had many victories in his life. He has also had his share of tragedies. His younger son, Clifford, was killed in a racing crash in 1992. In July of 1993, Allison lost his other son, Davey, in a fatal helicopter crash at the same Alabama track where he had watched Davey zoom to victory in 1987.

Bobby Allison, a NASCAR figure who gives much of his energy to charity, is one of the most winning drivers of all time. He has always loved speed. For many years, he flew his own Piper Aerostar planes. As a young boy, he almost drowned while testing a motorboat engine. It blew up a half mile from the shore, and Allison had to swim back in thirty-four-degree water.

Even though he loves speed, Bobby Allison usually won his races by being a careful driver, not a "banger" who ran other cars off the track. He was voted "Most Popular Driver" seven times in his racing career.

BOBBY ALLISON

BORN: December 3, 1937, Miami, Florida.

HIGH SCHOOL: Archbishop Curley High School, Miami, Florida.

RECORDS: Career total winnings of over $7 million.

By 1989, he was the leader in purses won at superspeedways.

Tied for third place on all-time NASCAR win list.

More than 600 short-track victories.

HONORS: Voted "Most Popular Driver" seven times.

IROC Series Champion—1980.

NASCAR Award of Excellence—1989.

Inducted into National Motorsports Hall of Fame—1993.

Olsonite Driver of the Year—1972, 1983.

Inducted into Eastern Motorsports Hall of Fame—1994.

Bobby Allison, known as a careful driver, took home over eighty wins, with a career total earnings of more than 7 million dollars.

NEIL BONNETT

Neil Bonnett's career ended tragically when he died in a crash at Daytona in February of 1994.

ENGINES ROARED. ON OCTOBER 11, 1987, thousands of fans dotted the stands at the Charlotte Motor Speedway. Some watched the race action. Others focused on the crowd around Neil Bonnett's Chevy. Emergency workers guided the Jaws of Life to cut away at Bonnett's car. The Chevy had become a metal prison. Bonnett sat trapped inside.

Emergency crews worked for twenty minutes before pulling Bonnett to safety. Later, Bonnett said, "I was in so much pain, I could hardly stand it. It had reached the point where I was wondering if I would lose my leg."[1]

Bonnett did not lose his leg and he did not stop racing. Still, he *did* warn others of the dangers. When Davey Allison wanted to get into the sport, Bonnett said, "Man, you don't need to get in this mess. . . . If you do this long enough, it'll bite you. . . . When somebody says, 'I'd like to go racing,' I tell them it's not just the day when you stand in victory lane waving to the crowd—there's other days . . . with your legs broken nearly off and a bunch of ribs caved into your lungs so you can't breathe."[2]

Even though Bonnett cautioned others, he had been "bitten." He couldn't take his own advice. After his 1987 injury, he fought hard to get back to racing. He worked out on special equipment. He promised to return to racing stronger and more determined.[3]

Bonnett's hard work and determination paid off. In 1988, he won back-to-back victories at the Pontiac Excitement 400 in Richmond, Virginia, and the Goodwrench 500 in Rockingham, North Carolina.

At Rockingham, Bonnett didn't lead until the 122nd lap. Then he sneaked past Dale Earnhardt, and he was out in front!

But Bonnett's pit stops were unusually slow. They sent him back into the action in fourth place toward the end of the race. Still, Bonnett led 176 of the last 371 laps. He grabbed a 0.62 win, just out in front of racer Lake Speed.

Bonnett had made a strong comeback. But his luck did not hold. A 1990 crash in Darlington, South Carolina, left him with memory loss due to head injuries. Doctors tried to convince him to leave racing, but Bonnett could not stay away. He said, "You can't walk away from the sport you've spent your entire life around."[4]

After someone else's 1993 crash at Talladega Superspeedway, Bonnett ran to pull racers from the twisted metal. He ignored the danger of leaking fuel. Oddly, the wreckage was not the result of a racing accident. Racers Red Farmer and Davey Allison had gone down in a helicopter crash.

Sadly, Allison did not survive his injuries. When Bonnett was praised for his actions, he did not take credit, saying only, "I just felt so helpless."[5]

In February 1994, Bonnett practiced for the Daytona 500. He had just left the thirty-one-degree banking in turn four when his Chevy skidded down the flat apron. Bonnett couldn't correct the skid. The Chevy slammed nose-first into the outside wall. Bonnett again became a prisoner trapped inside his car.

Once again, emergency crews cut away at the wreckage. But this time, no race to the emergency room could save Bonnett's life. Workers laid a tarp over the wreckage. Bonnett did not survive his massive head injuries.

Neil Bonnett, the man who had fought to come back, would race no more. Fans and racers remember his eighteen career victories and twenty pole positions. They still admire his courage, determination, and drive.

NEIL BONNETT

BORN: July 30, 1946, Hueytown, Alabama.

HIGH SCHOOL: Unknown.

RECORDS: In 1976, One top-5 and four top-10 finishes.

Career starts totaling 361.

Won back-to-back Busch Clashes—1983, 1984.

Won first NASCAR-style event ever held outside the United States–in Melbourne, Australia.

Neil Bonnett races at Daytona.

SARA CHRISTIAN

In October of 1949, Sara Christian did what no other woman had ever done. She finished in the top 5 in a NASCAR race, coming in only ten laps behind the winner.

"WHERE THE FASTEST THAT RUN, Run the Fastest." In 1949, this slogan spoke for the new sport of stock car racing. The group that managed the sport was called the "National Championship Stock Car Circuit," but founder Bill France wanted a new name and a new organization to manage the new sport of stock car racing. He thought of the "Stock Car Auto Racing Society," but he didn't want an organization called SCARS. NASCAR seemed to work just fine, though. The National Association for Stock Car Auto Racing set its first race for June 19, 1949. The purse was $5,000.

Sara Christian stood out as the leading woman stock car driver in the country in 1949. She had had no trouble qualifying for the June 19 race. Christian said that she had loved the sport from the time she had driven a race car for a promoter in 1947. Some said that she had been around stock car racing since the early days, before World War II. Back then, racers zipped around barrels set out on Florida beaches.

On June 19, 1949, Sara Christian sat behind the wheel of her '47 Ford, waiting to take to the dirt track in NASCAR's first official race. Over 13,000 people paid to see the race that day. Fans there saw something different from the sight at today's races. There was no rainbow of race car colors. Sponsor logos did not appear across the sides of the cars. Instead, most of the cars were black or gray. They included some of today's makes, like Buick, Mercury, Lincoln, Oldsmobile, Cadillac, Chrysler, and Ford. They also included makes that are no longer around, such as the Kaiser and Hudson.

The cars at the first official NASCAR race looked clunky

by today's standards. Still, on June 19, 1949, NASCAR was about to take off.

When the green flag waved, racers sped toward the first turn. Fans cheered. Engines roared. Dust rose into the air.

Then cars crashed. Oil dripped. Engines smoked.

After thirty grueling miles, Bob Flock relieved Christian. With Flock at the wheel, the engine on Christian's Ford overheated. It ended up in fourteenth place, a $50 finish. Sara Christian had been a part of the first NASCAR race in history.

Later in 1949, at the Strictly Stock Race Number 4 in Langhorne, Pennsylvania, Sarah Christian ran with famous racers like Curtis Turner, Bob Flock, and Red Byron. She finished sixth in the 200-lap run. Because of her outstanding performance, Christian was invited to join first-place finisher Curtis Turner in the winner's circle.

"She is so talented and so nerveless that she rode over cars who blocked her way."[1] That's what people had to say about Christian's track action.

In October 1949, Sara Christian did what no other woman has ever done. She finished in the top five in a NASCAR race, coming in ten laps behind winner Lee Petty. The race lasted 1 hour, 44 minutes, and 25.42 seconds, with an average speed of 57.458 miles per hour.

But Christian could not escape the danger faced by all NASCAR racers. In 1949 she suffered from a serious back injury, two fractured vertebrae, after a race at Lakewood Park in Atlanta, Georgia.

Still, in the 1949 NASCAR season, Sara Christian finished thirteenth, once in the top 5 and twice in the top 10. No woman has ever equaled her NASCAR record.

SARA CHRISTIAN

BORN: Unknown.

HIGH SCHOOL: Unknown.

RECORDS: Only woman to finish once in the the top 5 and twice in the top 10.

Honors: In 1949, the top female NASCAR driver in the country. Participant in the first NASCAR race in history.

Sara Christian's car looks big and clunky when compared to the more sleek NASCAR models of today.

BILL ELLIOTT

"Awesome Bill from Dawsonville," as Bill Elliott is known, has been voted Most Popular Driver many times. His career earnings total more than 13 million dollars.

A MILLION-DOLLAR BONUS! At the beginning of the 1985 season, the R. J. Reynolds company promised a one million-dollar bonus to any winner of three of the Big Four races: the Daytona 500, Talladega's Winston 500, Charlotte's World 600, and Darlington's Southern 500.

On January 2, 1985, Bill Elliott tested his new Ford Thunderbird at Daytona. No one's numbers even came close to his 202.893 mile per hour lap. During qualifications, Elliott won the pole with his shocking 205.114 miles per hour.

Shortly into the race, Elliott and Cale Yarborough dueled for first, but not for long. Yarborough's engine couldn't take the torture. It blew on the sixty-second lap. On lap 145, Elliott pitted for a tire change and fuel. He was set to return to the action in less than twenty seconds. Then officials ordered the pit crew to tape the right front headlight panel.

Elliott charged back to the field after a 41.19-second stop, but he trailed Neil Bonnett by more than a straightaway. Fans cheered when Elliott sped back into first after eleven laps.

One by one, racing engines began to blow. The punishing speeds were too much. A. J. Foyt, Bobby Allison, Harry Gant, Dale Earnhardt, Benny Parsons, Terry Labonte, and Neil Bonnett all dropped out of the action. No one could stand up to Elliott. He zoomed under the checkered flag to claim the first leg of the Winston Million.

After Elliott's Daytona victory, officials changed the rules about roof height. All cars would now run with roof heights of 50.5 inches. Some believed that Elliott had posted his stunning victory because of the low roof on his Thunderbird. He was forced to raise it.

Elliott qualified at Talladega with a roof height of 50.5 inches—and a speed of 209.398 miles per hour. Nothing could slow him down. He ran to a victory. One more win and Elliott would be one million dollars richer!

But Elliott couldn't hold on in Charlotte. His brakes failed. He ended up in eighteenth place, and the win went to Darrell Waltrip.

At Darlington, Elliott faced his last chance. He did not fail. Starting from the pole, Elliott was on again in Darlington at the Southern 500! He won the million!

Elliott had started on the road to the million back in his teenage years. His father, George, bought cars and raced them. But the family couldn't really afford the kind of cars they needed for NASCAR racing.

Bill Elliott's dad paid him for working on cars the family owned. Elliott also got jobs working on other racers' cars. Before he even graduated from high school, he had made some impressive dirt track runs.

Later, Elliott's father became a Ford dealer, and the family was able to afford better quality cars. The Elliotts finally had a car that finished in the top thirty-five at Rockingham. In 1981, the Elliotts found a sponsor, and Bill's professional racing career had truly begun.

Bill Elliott doesn't confine his flying to the race track. He also soars across the sky and does tricks in his aerobatic plane. He has a Cessna that he flies for business.

Elliott loves being behind the wheel, and he's certainly made his mark on the track. In 1985, Bill Elliott set records as the fastest driver in NASCAR history and the driver to win the most money. His season total that year was over two million dollars.

Today, he has a new nickname, one that he worked hard to earn: "Million Dollar Bill."

BILL ELLIOTT

BORN: October 8, 1955, Cumming, Georgia.

HIGH SCHOOL: Dawson County High School, Dawsonville, Georgia.

RECORDS: Won million dollar Winston Bonus in 1985; Set pole records at all Winston Cup Superspeedways; Had fastest qualifying speed in Winston Cup history—lap of 212.809 at Talladega, 1987; By 1989, he was the fastest NASCAR driver.

HONORS: Most Popular Driver, 1984, 1985, 1986, 1987, 1988, 1991, 1992, 1993, 1994, 1995, 1996, 1997; Inducted into Georgia Sports Hall of Fame, 1998.

Bill Elliott's pit crew races against time to make needed repairs and to get the car back on the track.

STERLING MARLIN

Sterling Marlin stands proudly with his trophy after winning the Daytona 500 in 1994.

SOME SAY IT WAS THE most competitive race in the history of the Daytona 500. On February 20, 1994, thirteen drivers went through thirty-three leader changes in 200 laps.

Who would take home the win? Screaming fans in the stands may have thought the trip down victory lane would belong to Dale Earnhardt that day. He was leading into lap 141. Then, with a yellow caution flag and about fifty laps remaining, Earnhardt, Jeff Gordon, and Ernie Irvan, along with most of the leaders, pitted for fuel.

Sterling Marlin and Mark Martin, also front-runners, elected not to pit. By lap 180, Irvan led, his seventh time to lead in eighty-four laps. But he got loose and dropped back to seventh.

On lap 182, Earnhardt was running third when handling problems slowed him down and finally snatched victory away. By the last two laps, Marlin, Irvan, and Martin dueled for top honors.

Then Martin ran dry and limped out of contention. Marlin was relieved. "I breathed a little easier when I saw Mark go dry. I knew if the three of us raced to the finish, the Fords (Martin and Irvan) would gang up on me. I figured I could beat them one-on-one."[1]

The checkered flag lay five miles ahead. Nearly 150,000 fans shouted in the stands. Would Marlin run dry just as Martin had? After all, neither Martin nor Marlin had decided to pit for fuel, and Martin had dropped out of the action as a result.

But Marlin held on. He zipped under the checkered flag

with Irvan breathing down his neck. Irvan took second just 0.23 seconds behind.

It had been a long time since 1983 when Marlin had been voted Rookie of the Year in his first full Winston Cup schedule. He had been fighting to come up with a win ever since. This made his Daytona 500 Victory especially sweet.

Sterling isn't the only Marlin to ever take to the track. His dad, Clifton B. Marlin, known as "Coo Coo," was behind the wheel in the very early years of stock car racing. Coo Coo was not as famous as racers like Lee Petty or Bobby Allison, but he introduced Sterling to racing at an early age.

When Sterling Marlin was a teenager, he played quarterback for his high school football team but still found time for racing. In 1982, he was voted Most Popular Driver in the Grand American Division.[2]

By 1989, he was involved in racing both on and off the track. When off the track, he wrote a newspaper column about racing. He was also still working with his father. The two had bought a 700-acre ranch in Tennessee which boasted tobacco and cattle.

Still, Sterling Marlin continued to race, always reaching for a Winston Cup win. In 1994, with determination and drive, he finally won the Daytona 500, "the Super Bowl of stock car racing."[3]

Once across the finish line, Marlin stopped to trade high-fives with pit crews. He ran out of fuel on his way to the victory circle, but he hadn't run out of fuel in his own personal race for first.

STERLING MARLIN

BORN: June 30, 1957, Columbia, Tennessee.

HIGH SCHOOL: Spring Hill High School, Spring Hill, Tennessee.

RECORDS: First in runner-up, top-5 and top-10 finishes.

HONORS: Rookie of the Year—1983.

Most Popular Driver in Grand American Division—1982.

Won Transouty Financial 400—1995.

Daytona 500 winner Sterling Marlin zips under the checkered flag.

BENNY PARSONS

Race fans have watched Benny Parsons on the track, and listened to his sports commentary on television for years.

BENNY PARSONS LOOKS AS NATURAL behind the camera as he does behind the wheel. As a commentator for ESPN, Parsons can describe races as well as run them. "He may be the best-liked driver on the track."[1]

Parsons is in a good position to talk about races and record-holders. He's set some impressive records himself. By 1987, he was one of only six drivers who had won the Daytona 500 *and* the Winston Cup. His career has already netted him purses worth almost 4 million dollars. In 1976 and 1977, he came in third in the Winston Cup Grand National Series. The only two who could top him those years were Cale Yarborough and Richard Petty.

The 1977 season was a big money-winning season for Parsons. He won one victory, the NAPA National 500, after running out of gas! Parsons ran out of fuel forty-seven laps before the finish. He had made a mistake in planning, and he didn't hear his crew chief radio him to pit for gas.

Parsons had been leading for most of the race when he ran out of fuel and had to pit. Yarborough saw a golden opportunity. He zipped out in front. But he couldn't hold the lead. Parsons outran him to finish first. It's a rare racer who can run out of gas and still make a trip to the winner's circle.

On July 31, Parsons snatched the Coca-Cola 500 from Richard Petty at Pocono International Raceway. With fifteen laps to go, Parsons held a two-second lead. "I knew I had to go strong, and I knew I was in a battle with a guy who doesn't lose too many of them. I had to be very careful that I didn't make any mistakes. There's always that gnawing fear that Richard has held something back for the finish."[2]

After taking second to Parsons, Petty said, "I just flat got outrun. Benny could go wherever he wanted to."[3]

Parsons, who earned $359,341 in 1977, couldn't stop thinking about having so much when others had so little. A tradition was born. Parsons began his Christmas parties for the underprivileged, and he has continued them ever since.[4]

Parsons' racing career began after he had dropped out of college. He took many jobs where he worked with cars, but he just couldn't decide exactly what he wanted to do with his life.[5]

One day, while Parsons was working at the gas pumps at his father's station, two men drove up. Parsons saw the race car on their trailer. They invited him to join them for a race. Parsons has been interested in racing ever since.

Even at age forty-five, Parsons ran a full season. He made over a half-million dollars for his team.

By 1992, Parsons had opened his own auto parts store. He remains one of the most down-to-earth racers, and race fans enjoy listening to him as he broadcasts on ESPN about the sport he loves so much.

BENNY PARSONS

BORN: July 12, 1941, Parsonsville, North Carolina.

HIGH SCHOOL: West Wilkes High School, North Wilkesboro, North Carolina.

RECORDS: By 1987, he was one of six drivers to win Winston Cup and Daytona 500.

HONORS: Winner of first Alan Kulwicki Award.

Automobile Racing Club of America Rookie of the Year—1965.

ARCA Champion—1968, 1969.

First ARCA Champion Inducted into International Motor Sports Hall of Fame—1994.

ACE Award Winner.

Benny Parsons takes to the track at Daytona.

RICHARD PETTY

Richard Petty won his first superspeedway race at age twenty-six. He went on to a record of two hundred wins.

IN **1992, PRESIDENT BUSH AWARDED** the Medal of Freedom, the highest U.S. civilian honor, to "some of our finest Americans."[1] Ten people received the medal. They included former talk-show host Johnny Carson, singer Ella Fitzgerald, actress Audrey Hepburn, author Elie Wiesel, and a NASCAR racer—the legendary Richard Petty.

Petty set many NASCAR records. He won 200 races, including seven Daytona 500s and seven championships. He was the first driver who earned $1 million, the first who earned $2 million, then $3 million, all the way up to $5 million. Petty is loved and admired by Americans not only for his skill on the track, but also because he treats his fans like gold. "One by one, hour by hour, day by day, since 1958, he has not only shaken their hands and signed their picture postcards, but he has also talked to them—'talked to me just like I was *somebody*,' as so many have said so often."[2]

"For 35 years he has signed his name, on average, 600 times a day . . . he signs posters, souvenirs, letters, trading cards, toys. He personally signs every response to every letter in the full mailbag that arrives every day at his racing compound . . ."[3]

In February 1964, Petty ran and won his first Daytona 500 at age twenty-six. He stormed the field, leading in all but sixteen laps. Averaging a record 154.334 miles per hour, Petty cruised into the lead on the fifty-second lap. He left the other racers choking on his dust. No one could touch him. Petty sailed under the checkered flag and took home $33,300 in winnings. This first superspeedway win was a sign of things to come in Petty's career.

In 1967, Petty took victory twenty-seven times, with ten consecutive wins. Along with Petty's record victories, his spectacular crash in the 1988 Daytona 500 holds a permanent place in NASCAR's scrapbook. This disaster is one of the most popular race scenes shown on film. At Daytona, Petty's Pontiac had just entered the fourth turn on the 106th lap. After a mishap with another racer, Petty began to spin. A.J. Foyt's Oldsmobile clipped Petty's Pontiac. The back of Petty's car flew up into the air. Hitting the fence along the front stretch, Petty flipped twelve times. Other drivers, trying to avoid the disaster, wriggled across the front stretch. Close to the pit row entrance, Petty's Pontiac finally settled down. Wham! Brett Bodine's Ford smashed into Petty.

Petty survived the crash with no serious injuries. Fans may have wondered that day whether their hero was made of steel. He has certainly shown his strength time and time again on the track.

On November 14, 1992, in the Georgia Dome, Richard Petty made a farewell appearance in front of a crowd of 75,000. He had come a long way since his first race on a dirt track in South Carolina in 1958. Petty is now a car owner and he supports, both with donations and his time, many charities, including the Brenner Children's Hospital in Winston-Salem, North Carolina.

Darrell Waltrip says about Petty, "Nobody fills those shoes . . . Richard was made for this sport, or this sport was made for Richard—however you want to look at it."[4]

RICHARD PETTY

BORN: July 2, 1937, Level Cross, North Carolina.

HIGH SCHOOL: Randleman High School, Randleman, North Carolina.

RECORDS: 200 Winston Cup victories.

Competed in 513 consecutive Winston Cup races.

Started in more than 1000 Winston Cup races.

First driver to earn $1, 2, 3, 4 and 5 million.

Winston Cup Champion—1964, 1967, 1971, 1972, 1974, 1975, 1979.

Career total winnings over $7 million.

Won $531,292 in a single season—1979.

HONORS: Rookie of the Year—1959.

Awarded Medal of Freedom by President Bush.

NASCAR Most Popular Driver Award—1962, 1964, 1968, 1970, 1974, 1975, 1976, 1977, 1978.

Received NASCAR's Award of Excellence—1987.

Inducted into North Carolina Athletic Hall of Fame—1973.

Richard Petty, one of the fans' favorite drivers, gets ready to face the competion.

The nickname "Fireball" came from Roberts's days as a baseball pitcher at the University of Florida, where he was known for his fastball.

FIREBALL ROBERTS

1958–WHAT A YEAR FOR for Fireball Roberts! He missed forty-one of fifty-one races and still finished eleventh in the Grand National point standings. He led more than 1,200 of the 2,601 laps he drove that year.

Roberts showed his talent on the track time and time again. The Florida Sports Writers voted him Professional Athlete of the Year. This award had never before been given to a race car driver. Some say that Roberts and his fame saved NASCAR at a time when the races might have stopped altogether. Many of the NASCAR stars had been killed on the track or had left the sport, and stock car racing was losing popularity. Roberts gave the sport the boost it needed.

In the 1958 Raleigh 250, Roberts ran strong but had a heart-pounding mishap. With only fifteen laps remaining, Bobby Keck's Chevy blew its engine and spun out of control. Roberts and racer Bob Welborn zipped high to steer clear of the Chevy. Their bumpers locked! And they stayed locked until the main straight. Finally, Roberts broke loose. In an exciting race where the lead had changed eight times between seven drivers, Roberts scooted to a one-lap victory.

In the 1958 Southern 500 at Darlington, crashes surrounded Roberts. One car skidded backwards up onto the guard rail. An explosion rocked the track. Flames rose high. Another car met the same fate. On lap 136, pole-winner Eddie Pagan blew a tire. He smashed through the guard rail. The retaining barrier was in a shambles and could not be repaired during the race. Officials warned racers.

Even so, a short time later, a racer spun out and shot

through the opening. Still another driver crashed when he blazed into the mangled mass of metal on the track.

But the wild crashes couldn't stop Fireball Roberts. They didn't even slow him down. By the 169th lap, he was out in front. He sped to victory in the remaining 195 laps. The next car finished five laps behind.

Roberts's win set two records: a fifth superspeedway victory and a third victory in a row. He became a familiar face in the winner's circle and an important part of NASCAR history.

In 1958, Roberts raced first under the checkered flag in the Old Dominion 500 in Martinsville, Virginia. He drove to a victory on a flat tire! But even he admitted that he might not have won if the race had not been called at 350 laps because of darkness.

"Fireball had a lot of ability and he was very smart about a race car . . . he could take a slower race car and was able to win with it. And everyone recognized that."[1]

The nickname "Fireball" came from Roberts's days as a baseball pitcher at the University of Florida, where he was known for his fastball. It was especially ironic that he lost his life after a fiery crash in Charlotte, North Carolina, in 1964.

After Roberts's death and the death of racer Joe Weatherly, NASCAR began to enforce stronger safety measures. Today, sections in the stands at Daytona are named after Fireball Roberts and other greats who have lost their lives as the result of racing accidents.

FIREBALL ROBERTS

BORN: January 20, 1929.

HIGH SCHOOL: Apotka High School.

RECORDS: By 1958, he was the first to win five Superspeedway victories and to have three consecutive victories.

HONORS: Florida Sportswriters' Professional Athlete of the Year— 1958.

A section of the Daytona International Speedway stands is named in his honor.

After Fireball Roberts's death on the track in 1964, NASCAR began to enforce stronger safety measures.

DARRELL WALTRIP

By 1989, Darrell Waltrip had become the highest-paid driver in NASCAR history.

DARRELL WALTRIP

"**I Won The Daytona 500!** . . . I can't believe I won it! . . . I'm not dreamin', am I?"[1] Darrell Waltrip radioed his crew during his cool-off lap in 1989 at Daytona.

Before his big 1989 Daytona win, Darrell Waltrip had seventy-three NASCAR victories under his belt. Even so, Daytona was the one that had gotten away each and every year, time and time again. But in 1989, Daytona couldn't keep Waltrip out of victory lane. His determination to be first under the checkered flag finally paid off.

How did he win? Strategy! When the cars first snaked out onto the track, Waltrip was calm, cool, and collected. Fifty laps later, Geoff Bodine, Ken Schrader, Dale Earnhardt, and Waltrip dueled for the lead. All drove Monte Carlos.

With fifty-three laps remaining, Waltrip pitted for fuel. After eighteen more laps, in seventh place, he radioed his crew. He thought he was getting better mileage than the other drivers. He didn't want to pit again for gas. His crew chief didn't agree with him.

But Waltrip insisted. "It's the only way we can win. I can make it. I *promise* I can make it!"[2]

Waltrip didn't stop. Eighty miles stretched out between his Monte Carlo and the checkered flag. He'd have to be light on the pedal and drive in the wake of other drivers. Schrader had scooted into the lead.

Twenty-five laps later, Earnhardt and Schrader pitted for gas one last time. They flew out of the pits and came up third and fourth behind leader Waltrip and Alan Kulwicki.

Engine trouble forced Earnhardt into the pits. Kulwicki dropped out with a cut tire four laps before the finish. Waltrip ran in the lead by eight seconds! He zoomed down the track, racing toward the finish! Then he checked his gas gauge. "I'm out! I'm out!" he frantically radioed his pit crew.

"Shake it, baby, shake it! Shake it, baby, shake it!"[3] a voice shot back. Waltrip's crew chief wanted Waltrip to swerve around to make any extra fuel spill into the line.

Waltrip blazed down the track. His gauge showed his tank was empty. Even so, he forged ahead, the first to sail under the checkered flag on his way to victory lane. Guts and glory were his.

Waltrip's racing career began when he finished high school. He had been popular in school, where he played on the football team.

When he finished high school, he took to the track. By the time he was twenty-five, he was racing on the top circuit. And at the age of twenty-eight, he took his first big win. Waltrip had only just started a career that would put him in NASCAR's record books. By 1989, Darrell Waltrip had become the highest-paid driver in NASCAR history.

Waltrip is sharp and well-spoken, often using his comments to confuse other drivers and to break their concentration. He contributes to charities, and has spoken on television against drug abuse.

DARRELL WALTRIP

BORN: January 5, 1947, Owensboro, Kentucky.

HIGH SCHOOL: Davies County High School, Owensboro, Kentucky.

RECORDS: First Winston Cup Driver to earn $6, 7, 8, 9, and 10 million.

Has eighty-four Winston Cup victories—tied for third with Bobby Allison.

Has twenty-three Superspeedway poles.

By 1995, he was the only driver to win $500,000 or more in a season fifteen times.

By 1995, he was the only 5-time winner of the Coca-Cola 600—1978, 1979, 1985, 1988, 1989.

Won a modern-era record of eight races from pole in 1981—tied all-time record of four consecutive.

By 1989, he had won more money than any other NASCAR driver.

HONORS: Most Popular Driver—1981, 1982, 1985.

American Driver of the Year—1979, 1981, 1982.

National Motorsports Press Association Driver of the Year—1977, 1981, 1982.

Auto Racing Digest Driver of the Year—1981, 1982.

Tennessee Professional Athlete of the Year—1979.

Darrell Waltrip leads the pack.

position belongs to the car and not the driver, Ricky Rudd took the pole with a 198.864 mile-per-hour lap.

When the green flag fell, Yarborough sped out driving a Pontiac Le Mans. After a hard-fought race, it all finally came down to the last twelve laps. Yarborough trailed Buddy Baker up until the last lap. Then he sneaked past Baker and left three cars fighting behind as he scampered to a five-car-length victory. Nothing could hold Yarborough back.

Yarborough's determination is not limited to the track. He has been strong and independent from the time he was very young. Yarborough lost his father at the age of ten, and he became a "tough kid."[2] Opponents fell to him in the boxing ring as he fought his way up to become state Golden Gloves champion. And he was as comfortable wrestling with an alligator as he was wrestling with ball players on the high school football field.

Even though Yarborough was offered a football scholarship to college, he turned it down. "All he wanted to do was race cars."[3]

Yarborough's racing career did not come easily to him. He took odd jobs for years until he finally became a professional driver. His patience paid off. Today, he owns race cars, a farm, restaurants, car dealerships, and other businesses.

Yarborough is a racing legend. Some call him "the most aggressive race car driver of them all."[4]

CALE YARBOROUGH

BORN: March 27, 1940, Sardis, South Carolina.

HIGH SCHOOL: Timmonsville High School, Timmonsville, South Carolina.

RECORDS: Won three consecutive Winston Cup Championships.

Is a 5-time winner of Southern 500.

First driver to win three consecutive Winston Cup titles.

Cale Yarborough drove his way to more than eighty wins, with total career earnings of over 5 million dollars.

NOTES BY CHAPTER

Bobby Allison

1. Gregory Lawrence Fielden, *Forty Years of Stock Car Racing*, Volume III, "Big Bucks and Boycotts, 1965-71," (Surfside Beach, S.C.: Garfield Press, 1990), p. 91.

2. Gregory Lawrence Fielden, *Forty Years of Stock Car Racing, The Modern Era, 1972-1989*, Volume IV, (Surfside Beach, S.C.: Garfield Press, 1990), p. 12.

Neil Bonnett

1. George H. Gilliam, *Racin': The NASCAR/Winston Cup Stock Racing Series*, (Charlottesville, VA: Howell Press, Inc., 1992), p. 87.

2. Ed Hinton, "Upfront: Remembering Neil Bonnett," *Car and Driver*, May, 1994, p. 40

3. Gilliam, p. 88.

4. "Bonnett Dies Pursuing His Passion," *Houston Chronicle*, February 12, 1994.

5. Hinton, p. 40

Sara Christian

1. Robert Cutter and Bob Fendell, *Encyclopedia of Auto Racing Greats*, (New York: Prentice-Hall, 1973), p. 132.

Bill Elliott

No notes.

Sterling Marlin

1. "Marlin snaps Chain, Wins Daytona 500," *Houston Chronicle*, February 21, 1994.

2. George H. Gilliam, *Racin': The NASCAR/Winston Cup Stock Racing Series*, (Charlottesville, VA: Howell Press, Inc., 1992), p. 98

3. "Marlin snaps Chain, Wins Daytona 500," *Houston Chronicle*, February 21, 1994.

Benny Parsons

1. George H. Gilliam, *Racin': The NASCAR/Winston Cup Stock Racing Series*, (Charlottesville, VA: Howell Press, Inc., 1992), p. 83.

2. Gregory Lawrence Fielden, *Forty Years of Stock Car Racing, The Modern Era, 1972-1989*, Volume IV, (Surfside Beach, S.C.: The Garfield Press, 1990, Third Printing, June 1992), pp. 203-204.

3. Ibid., p. 204.

4. Gilliam, p. 83.

5. Ibid.

Richard Petty

1. *Facts on File, World News Digest with Index*, v. 52, no. 2718.

2. Ed Hinton, "The King," *Sports Illustrated*, October 19, 1992, p. 66.

3. Ibid., p. 70.

4. Hinton, "The King", p. 70.

Fireball Roberts

1. Peter Golenbock, *American Zoom* (New York: Macmillan, 1993), p. 129.

Darrell Waltrip

1. Sam Moses, "About Time, Fella," *Sports Illustrated*, February 27, 1989, p. 47.

2. Ibid.

3. Ibid.

Cale Yarborough

1. George H. Gilliam, *Racin': The NASCAR/Winston Cup Stock Racing Series*, (Charlottesville, VA: Howell Press, Inc., 1992), p. 72.

2. Ibid.

3. Ibid.

4. Ibid.

INDEX